S0-ADR-716

Piano Lessons

Book 2

Authors
**Barbara Kreader, Fred Kern,
Phillip Keveren, Mona Rejino**

Consultants
Tony Caramia, Bruce Berr,
Richard Rejino

*Director,
Educational Keyboard Publications*
Margaret Otwell

Editor
Anne Wester

Illustrator
Fred Bell

FOREWORD

When music excites our interest and imagination, we eagerly put our hearts into learning it. The music in the **Hal Leonard Student Piano Library** encourages practice, progress, confidence, and best of all – success! Over 1,000 students and teachers in a nationwide test market responded with enthusiasm to the:

- variety of styles and moods
- natural rhythmic flow, singable melodies and lyrics
- "best ever" teacher accompaniments
- improvisations integrated throughout the **Lesson Books**
- orchestrated accompaniments included in audio and MIDI formats.

When new concepts have an immediate application to the music, the effort it takes to learn these skills seems worth it. Test market teachers and students were especially excited about the:

- "realistic" pacing that challenges without overwhelming
- clear and concise presentation of concepts that allows room for a teacher's individual approach
- uncluttered page layout that keeps the focus on the music.

The **Piano Practice Games** books are preparation activities to coordinate technique, concepts, and creativity with the actual music in **Piano Lessons**. In addition, the **Piano Theory Workbook** presents fun writing activities for review, and the **Piano Solos** series reinforces concepts with challenging performance repertoire.

The **Hal Leonard Student Piano Library** is the result of the efforts of many individuals. We extend our gratitude to all the teachers, students and colleagues who shared their energy and creative input. May this method guide your learning as you bring this music to life.

Best wishes,

Barbara Kreader   Fred Kern   Phillip Keveren   Mona Rejino

Book: ISBN 978-0-7935-6265-7
Book/Audio: ISBN 978-0-634-03119-9

HAL•LEONARD®
CORPORATION
7777 W. BLUEMOUND RD. P.O. BOX 13819 MILWAUKEE, WI 53213

Visit Hal Leonard Online at
www.halleonard.com

REVIEW OF BOOK ONE

THE GRAND STAFF

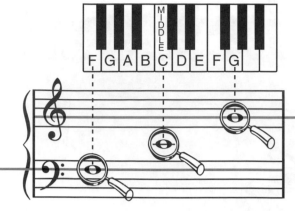

The **G note** is your reading guide for the **Treble or G Clef** (𝄞)

The **F note** is your reading guide for the **Bass or F Clef** (𝄢)

Middle C is your reading guide for the notes between the Treble and Bass Clefs.

NOTE VALUES

♩	quarter note	=	1 pulse	=	𝄽 quarter rest
𝅗𝅥	half note	=	2 pulses	=	▬ half rest
𝅗𝅥.	dotted half note	=	3 pulses		
𝅝	whole note	=	4 pulses		

DYNAMIC SIGNS tell how loudly or softly to play and help create the mood of the music.

p	(piano)	=	soft
mp	(mezzo piano)	=	medium soft
mf	(mezzo forte)	=	medium loud
f	(forte)	=	loud

MUSICAL TERMS

time signatures **4/4 3/4**

repeat sign :‖

D.C. (Da Capo) al Fine means to return to the beginning (capo) and play until you see the sign for the end (fine).

steps   skips   tied notes

TEMPO MARKS tell the mood of the piece and the speed of the pulse.

Adagio   Andante   Allegro
slowly   *walking speed*   *quickly*

CONTENTS

* Students can check pieces as they play them.

WHOLE REST

▬

means to rest for
an entire measure.

Remember,

Whenever you see
this magnifying glass,
fill in the name of the
note.

UNIT 1

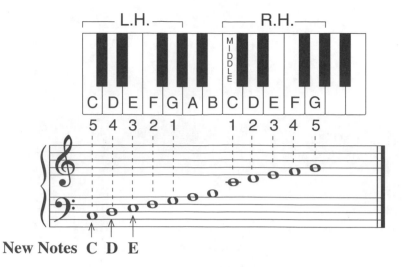

L.H.   R.H.

C D E F G A B C D E F G
5 4 3 2 1 1 2 3 4 5

MIDDLE

New Notes   C   D   E

Reflection

Moderately

Barbara Kreader

mp Am I the re - flec - tion in the mir - ror on the wall?

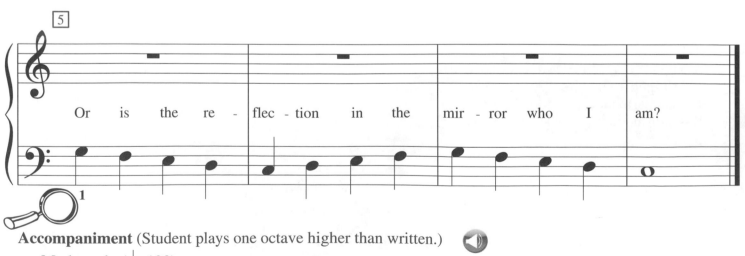

Or is the re - flec - tion in the mir - ror who I am?

Accompaniment (Student plays one octave higher than written.)

Moderately (♩=120)

p

My Own Song
On C D E F G

Place both hands on C D E F G. Listen and feel the pulse as your teacher plays the accompaniment below.

With your right hand, play C D E F G and then play G F E D C. Experiment by mixing the letters any way you want and make up your own song!

With your left hand, play C D E F G and then play G F E D C. Again, mix the letters any way you want and make up another song!

Have fun!

Accompaniment
Moderately (♩=120)

Repeat as necessary   *Last time*

Ode To Joy

Ludwig van Beethoven
(1770–1827)
Adapted by Fred Kern

With majesty

Accompaniment (Student plays one octave higher than written.)

With majesty (♩=105)

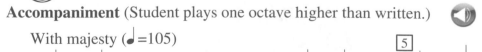

Carmen's Tune

Georges Bizet
(1838–1875)
Adapted by Fred Kern

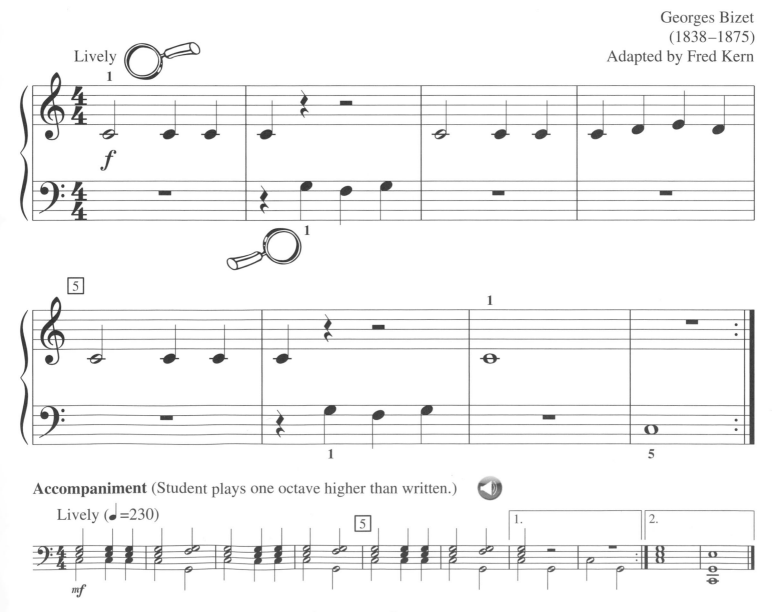

Accompaniment (Student plays one octave higher than written.)

Andantino

Louis Köhler
(1820–1886)
Adapted by Fred Kern

* *Andantino means a slightly faster tempo than Andante.*

Remember,

TIES

A **Tie** is a curved line that connects two notes of the same pitch. Hold one sound for the combined value of both notes.

Big Ben

Steady (♩=120)

Traditional

Hold down damper pedal throughout.

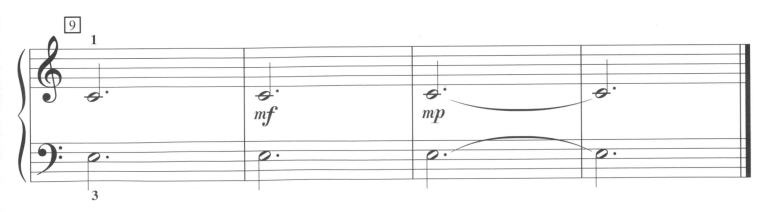

9

INTERVAL

An **Interval** is the distance from one key to another key.

Interval of a 2nd	Interval of a 3rd

Melodic Intervals – Notes played one after the other make a melody.
Harmonic Intervals – Notes played together make harmony.

With your left hand play:

Melodic 2nds   Harmonic 2nds   Melodic 3rds   Harmonic 3rds

Please, No Bees!

Cranky (♩=155)

Barbara Kreader

mf Please, no bees! Please, no bees on my nose or

neck or knees! Bring no sting! Bring no sting!

Find a rose, not my nose! Ouch! f

Lowest C on the piano.

10

Clapping Song

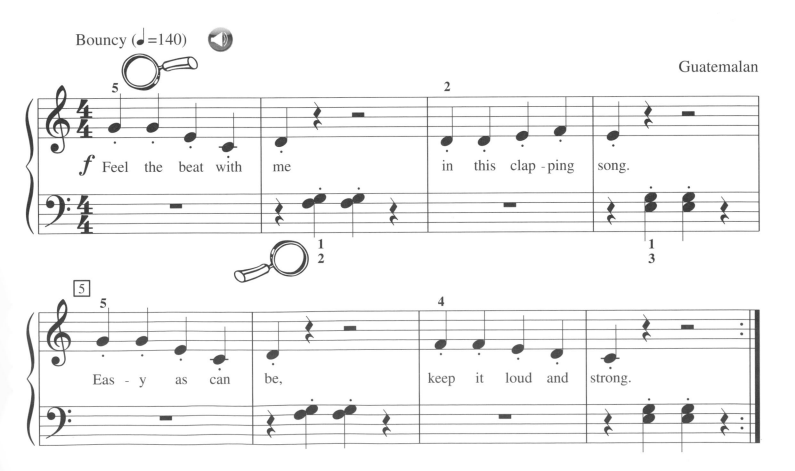

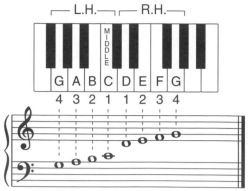

INTERVAL of a 4th

On the piano, a 4th
- skips two keys
- skips two fingers
- skips two letters

On the staff, a 4th
- skips two notes from either a line to a space or a space to a line.

Hoedown

Janet Medley

Toe tappin'

f At the hoe-down, do - si - do, all our friends will meet.

Swing your part - ner, don't be slow. Clap your hands and stomp your feet!

Accompaniment (Student plays one octave higher than written.)

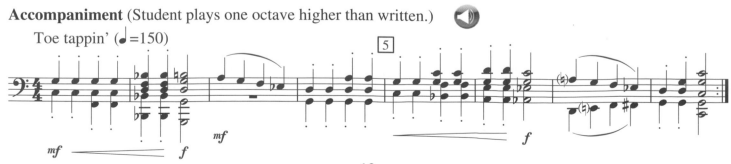

Toe tappin' (♩=150)

12

Sunlight Through The Trees

Flowing (♩=120)

Phillip Keveren

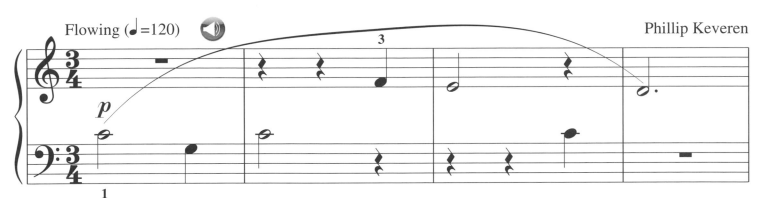

Play one octave higher than written and hold down damper pedal throughout.

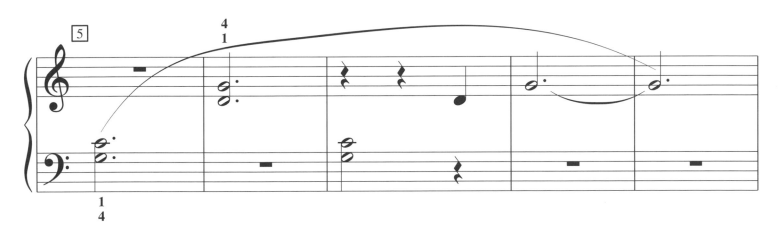

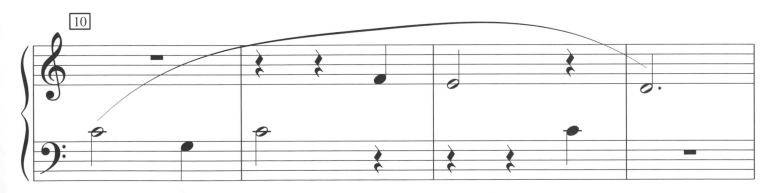

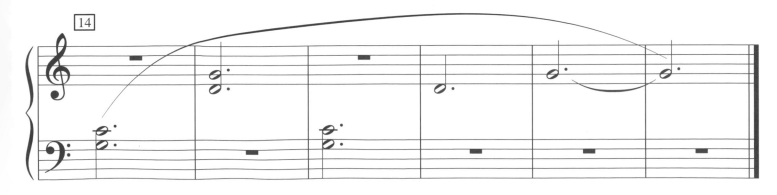

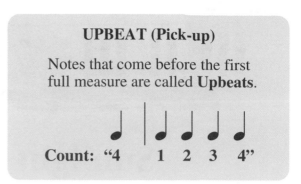

UPBEAT (Pick-up)

Notes that come before the first full measure are called **Upbeats**.

Count: "4   1   2   3   4"

Bingo

Bouncy

Traditional

mf Oh, once a farm-er had a dog and Bin-go was his name - o.

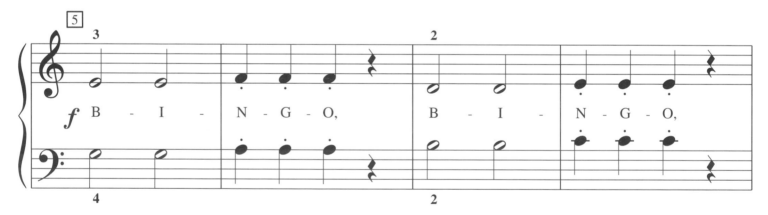

f B - I - N - G - O,   B - I - N - G - O,

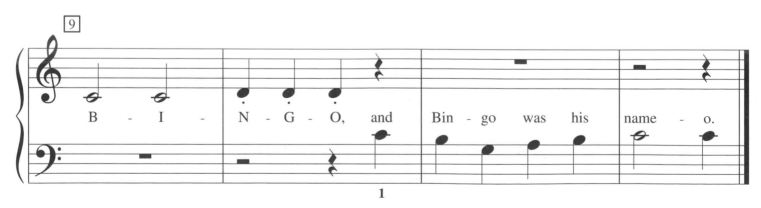

B - I - N - G - O, and Bin-go was his name - o.

Accompaniment (Student plays one octave higher than written.)

Bouncy (♩=140)

mp   *mf*

14

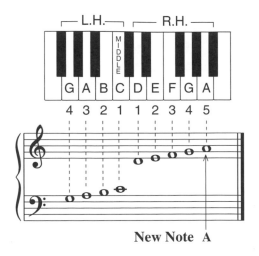

New Note A

Travelling Along
The Prairie

Italo Taranta

Accompaniment (Student plays one octave higher than written.)

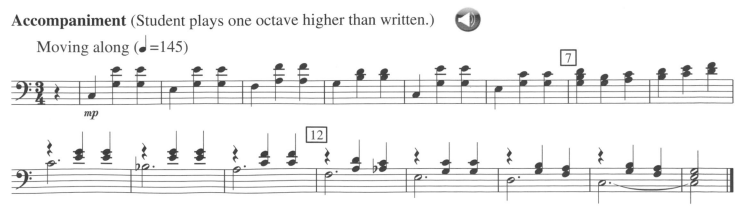

DYNAMIC SHADING is created by gradually changing from soft to loud or loud to soft.

Crescendo	Decrescendo
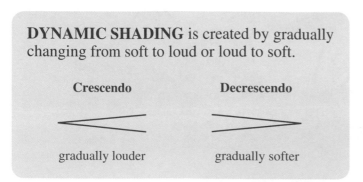	
gradually louder	gradually softer

No One To Walk With

Slowly

Italo Taranta

Accompaniment (Student plays one octave higher than written.)

Slowly ($\quad$=100)

16

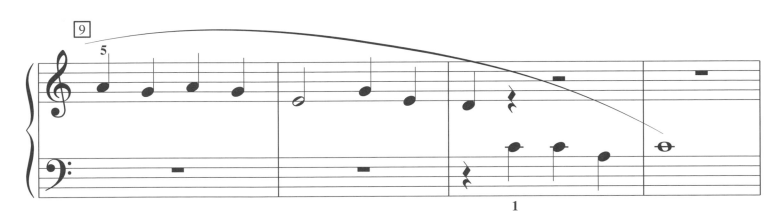

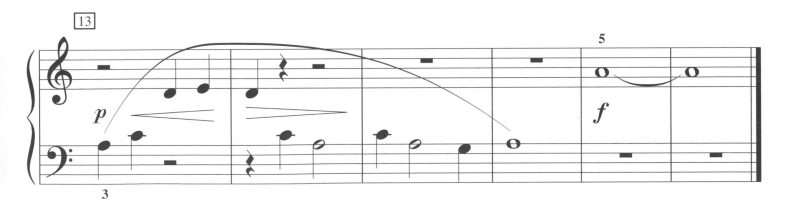

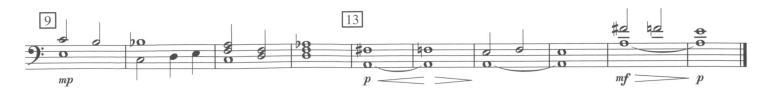

Painted Rocking Horse

Phillip Keveren

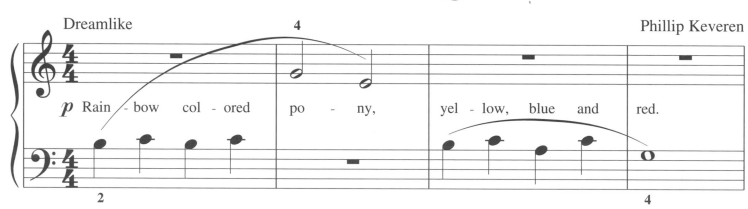

Dreamlike

p Rain - bow col - ored   po - ny,   yel - low, blue and   red.

Al - ways here be - side me,   stand - ing by my   bed.

Accompaniment (Student plays two octaves higher than written.)

Dreamlike ($\quad$=95)

With pedal

When the sky is cloud - y, you and I can play,

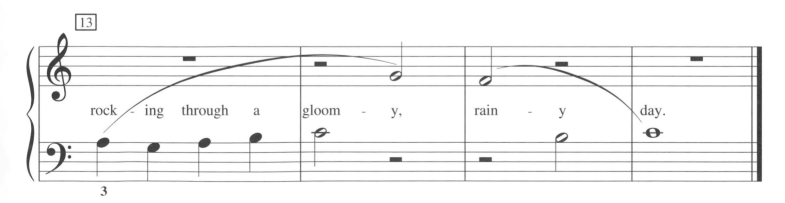

rock - ing through a gloom - y, rain - y day.

Tick Tock The Jazz Clock

With a steady beat like the tick of a clock

Bill Boyd

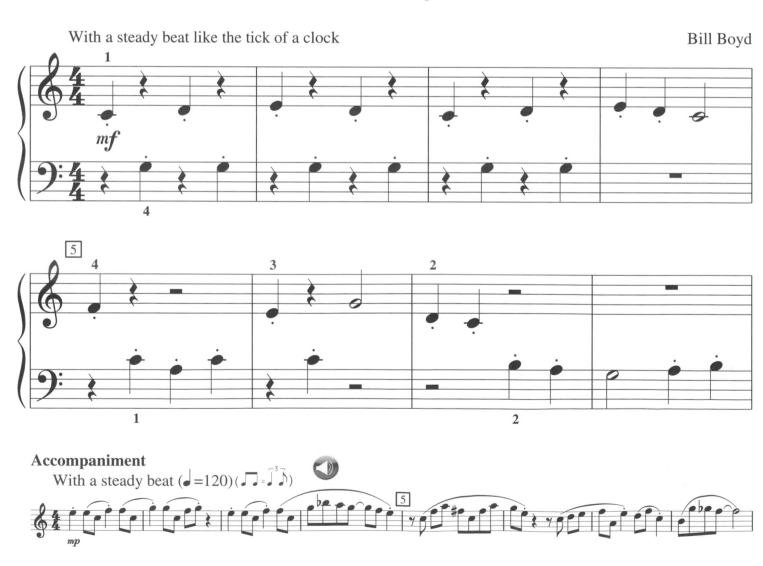

Accompaniment

With a steady beat (♩=120) (♫ = ♪♪)

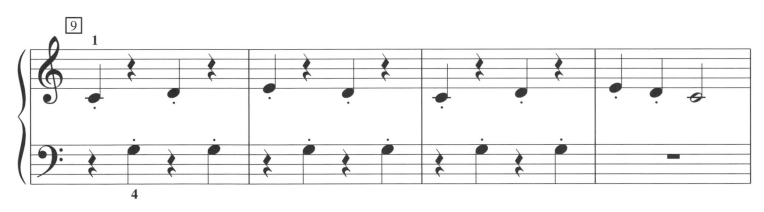

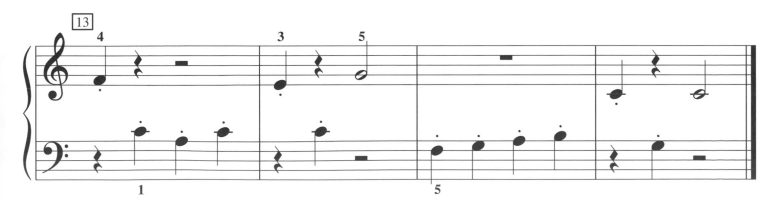

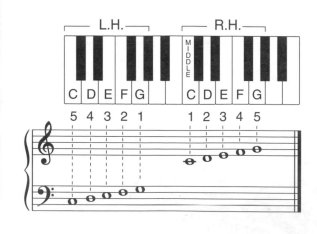

INTERVAL of a 5th

On the piano, a 5th
- skips three keys
- skips three fingers
- skips three letters

On the staff, a 5th
- skips three notes from either a line to a line or a space to a space.

Watercolors

Delicately (♩=105)

Phillip Keveren

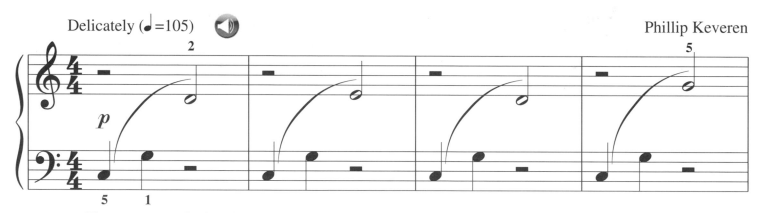

Play one octave higher than written and hold down damper pedal throughout.

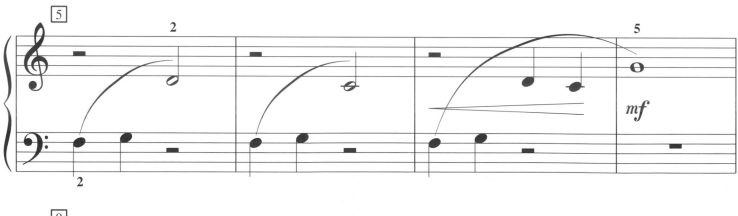

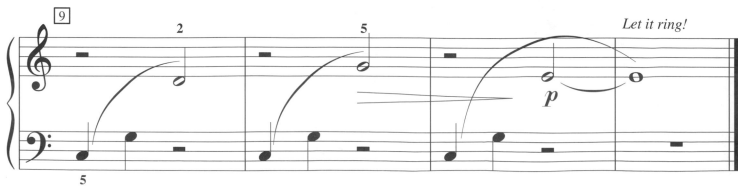

Circle Dance

Lively (♩=165)

Phillip Keveren

'Round in a cir - cle we spin to the mel - o - dy,

diz - zy and diz - zi - er, 'til we fall down!

Fine

mp

D.C. al Fine

23

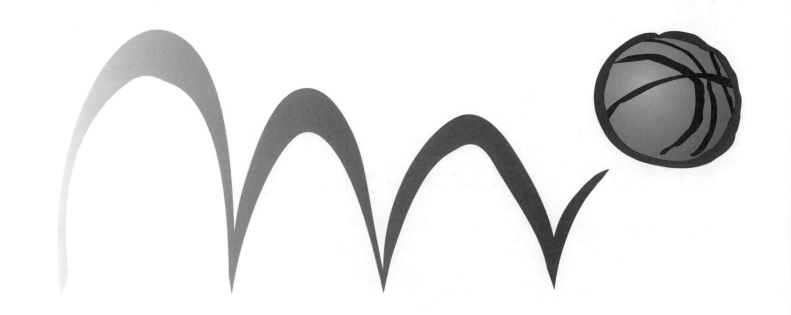

Basketball Bounce

Tempo de dribble (With energy!) (♩=190)

Phillip Keveren

Allegro

8va ---¬

When the sign *8va---¬* appears over a note or group of notes, play the note or notes one octave (eight notes) higher than written.

Anton Diabelli
(1781–1858)
Adapted by Fred Kern

8va - - -⌐

When the sign *8va* - - -⌐ appears under a note or group of notes, play the note or notes one octave lower than written.

Great News!

FORTISSIMO

ff

means very loud.

With excitement! (♩=170)

Bruce Berr

26

Brass Fanfare

Triumphantly (♩=110)

Phillip Keveren

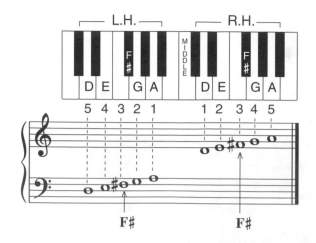

Little River Flowing

Smoothly

Folk Tune

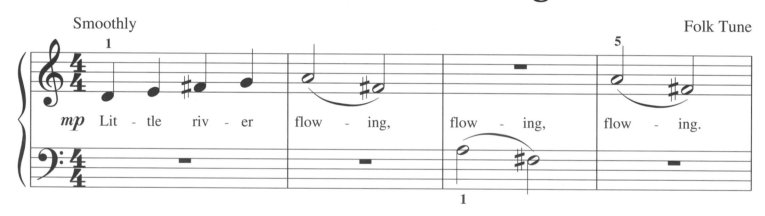

mp Lit - tle riv - er flow - ing, flow - ing, flow - ing.

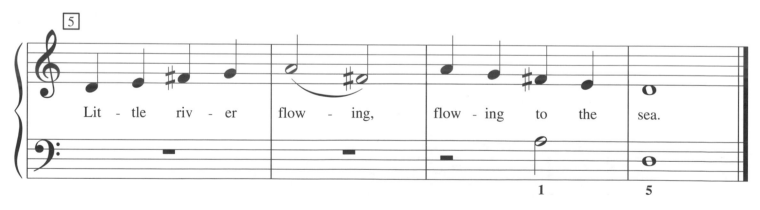

Lit - tle riv - er flow - ing, flow - ing to the sea.

Accompaniment (Student plays one octave higher than written.)

Smoothly (♩=145)

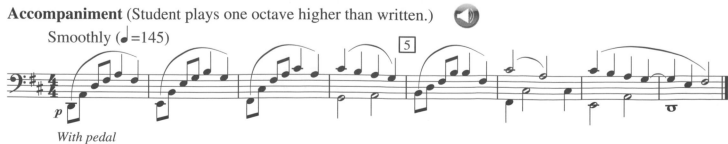

p

With pedal

28

Quiet Thoughts

H. Berens
(1826–1880)
Op. 62
Adapted by Fred Kern

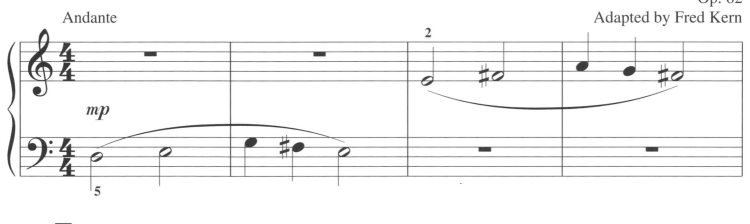

When a sharp appears before a note,
it remains sharp for one entire measure.

Accompaniment (Student plays one octave higher than written.)

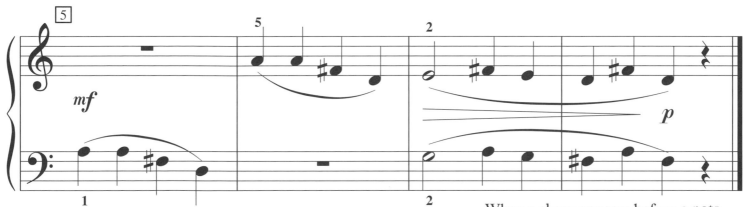

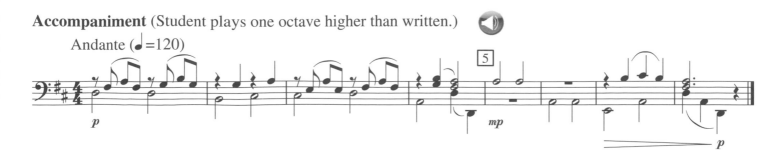

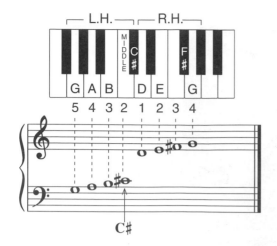

A B A Form

In "Star Quest," lines one and two are the A section, lines three and four are the B section. After B, you play A one more time.

The form of this piece is A B A.

Star Quest

A

Heroic March

Phillip Keveren

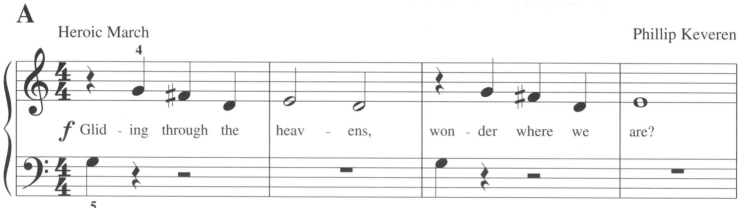

f Glid - ing through the heav - ens, won - der where we are?

Fine

Great ga - lac - tic trav - 'lers, search - ing for a star.

Accompaniment (Student plays one octave higher than written.)

Heroic March (♩ =120)

mf

Fine

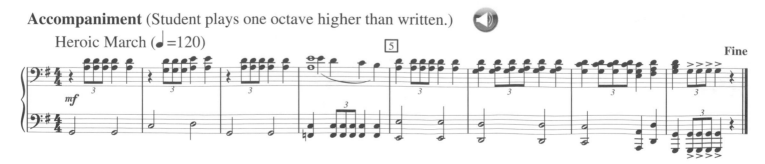

B

D.C. al Fine

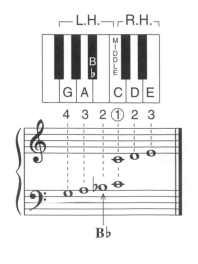

A Little Latin

Bill Boyd

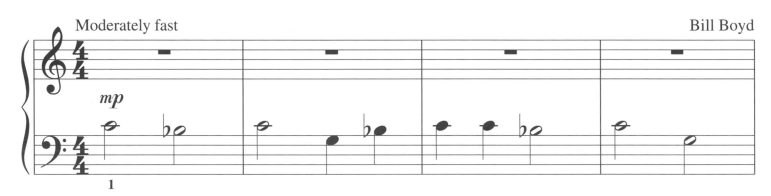

Moderately fast

mp

5

mf

f

Accompaniment (Student plays one octave higher than written.)

Moderately fast (♩=170)

p   *mp*   *mf*

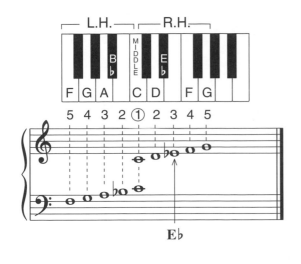

ACCENT

>

An **Accent** over or under a note means to play that note louder.

Stompin'

Keep the beat! (♩=190)

Bill Boyd

D♯ is the same piano key as E♭.

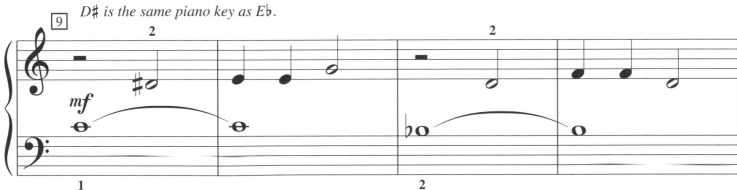

33

RITARD

Ritard or *rit.* means to slow the tempo gradually.

First Light

Gaelic Melody
Words by Fred Kern

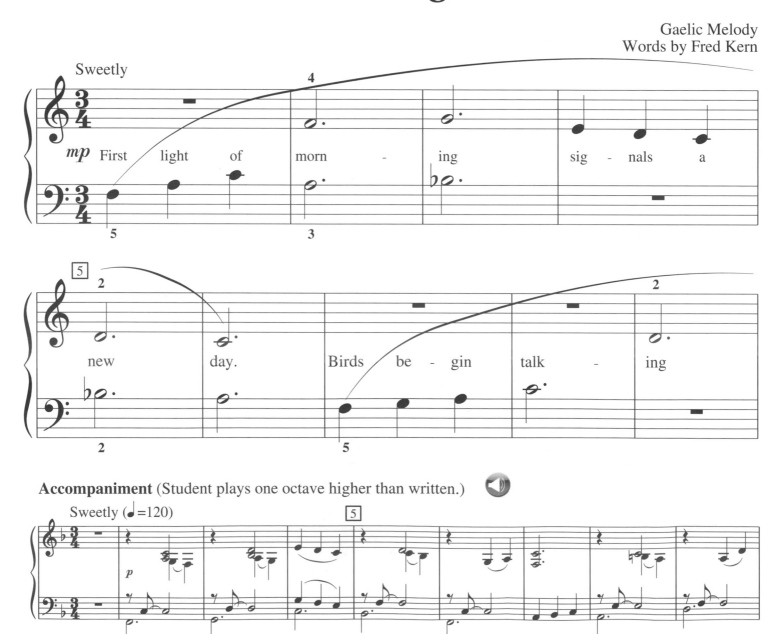

Accompaniment (Student plays one octave higher than written.)

Sweetly (♩=120)

Inspector Hound

Phillip Keveren

Sneaky (♩=145)

Lowest D on the piano

Bayou Blues

Phillip Keveren

Slow and bluesy (♩=110)

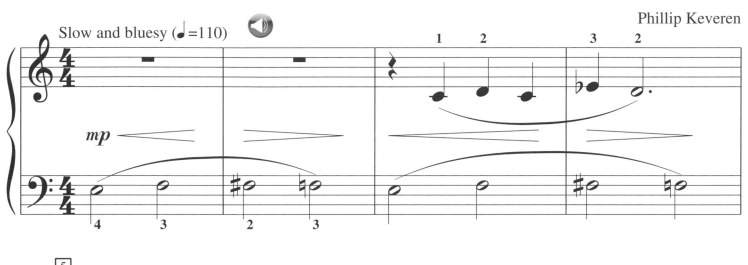

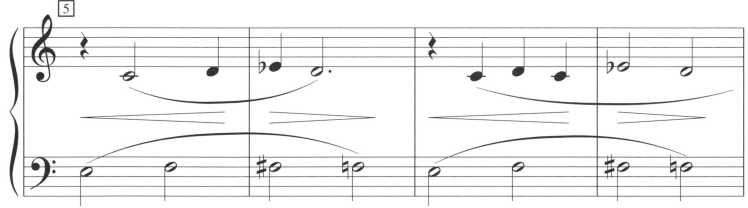

8va

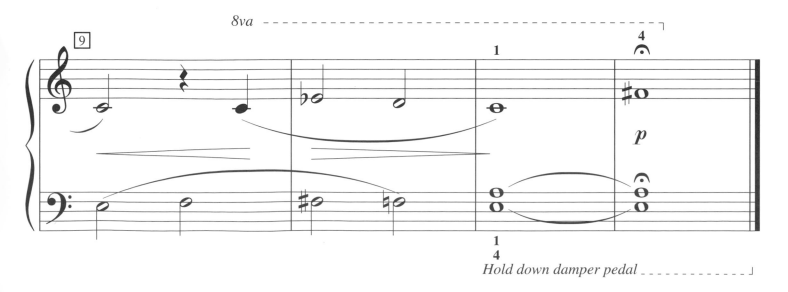

Hold down damper pedal

Serenade

Andante

Italo Taranta

Accompaniment (Student plays one octave higher than written.)

Andante (♩=145)

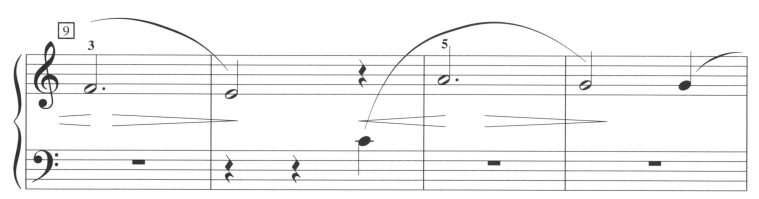

A sharp before a note
lasts for only one measure.

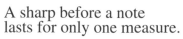

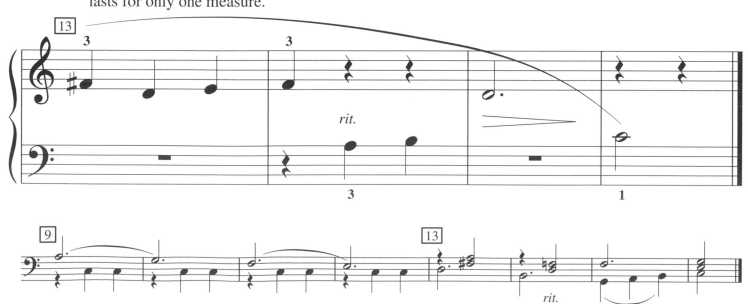

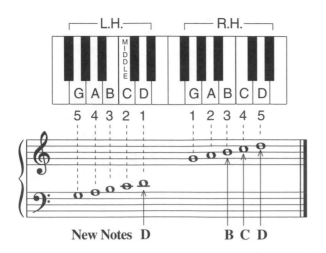

Ledger Lines are added when notes are written higher or lower than the staff.

Summer Evenings

"Alouette"
Words by Barbara Kreader

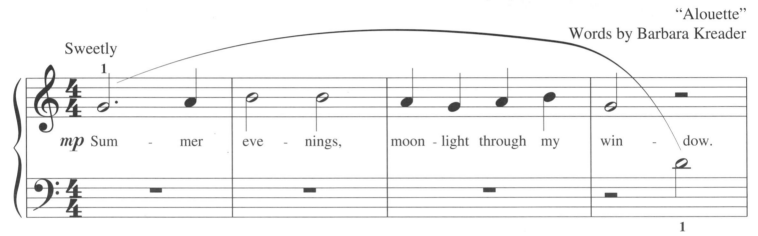

Sweetly

mp Sum — mer eve — nings, moon - light through my win — dow.

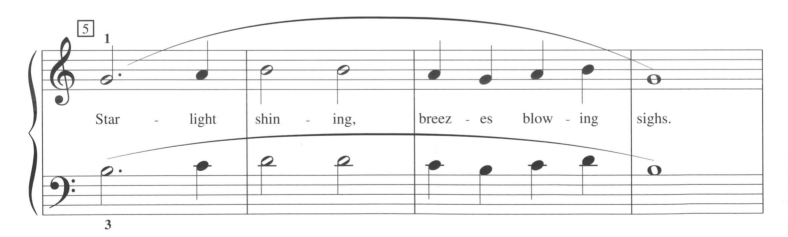

Star — light shin — ing, breez – es blow – ing sighs.

Accompaniment (Student plays one octave higher than written.)

Sweetly (♩=150)

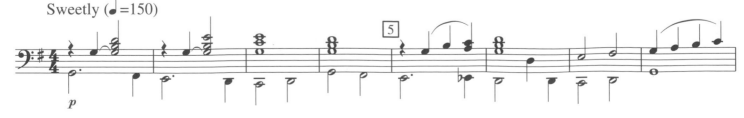

p

40

As I lie up - on my bed, sights and sounds soon fill my head.

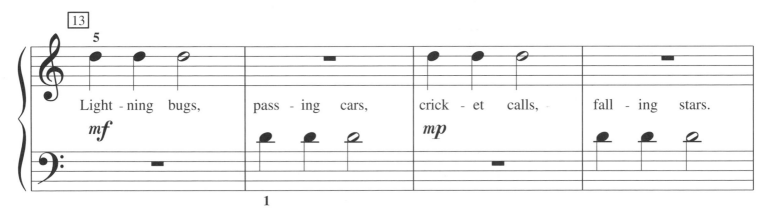

Light - ning bugs, pass - ing cars, crick - et calls, fall - ing stars.

mf *mp*

mf Sum - mer eve - nings warm and soft and still. *rit.*

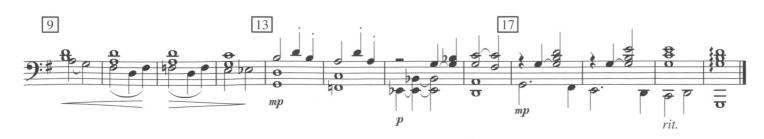

mp *p* *mp* *rit.*

My Own Song
On G A B C D

Place both hands on G A B C D. Listen and feel the pulse as your teacher plays the accompaniment below.

With your right hand, play G A B C D. Experiment by playing D C B A G. Mix the letters any way you want and make up your own song!

With your left hand, play G A B C D. Experiment by playing D C B A G. Again, mix the letters any way you want and make up another song!

Have fun!

Accompaniment

Jazz Waltz (♩=170)

Pop!

Bouncy (♩=200)

"Pop Goes The Weasel"

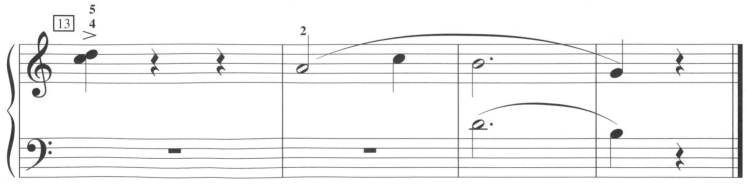

Go To Sleep

Andante

Folk Tune

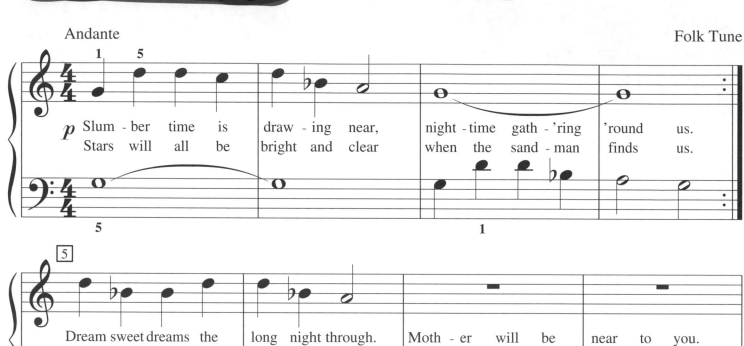

p Slum - ber time is draw - ing near, night - time gath - 'ring 'round us.
Stars will all be bright and clear when the sand - man finds us.

Dream sweet dreams the long night through. Moth - er will be near to you.

Go to sleep, my dear one. Go to sleep, my dear one.

pp rit.

Accompaniment (Student plays one octave higher than written.)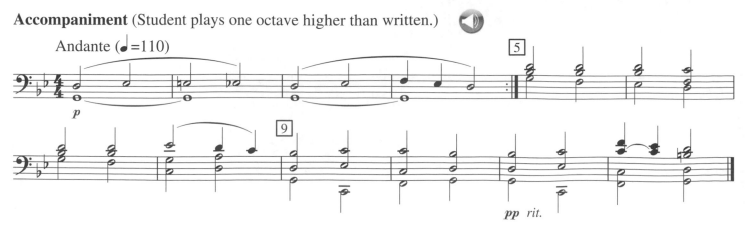

Andante (♩=110)

p

pp rit.

Jig

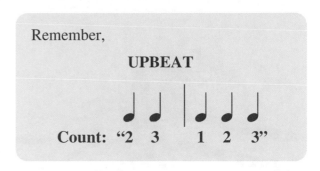

Remember,

UPBEAT

Count: "2 3 | 1 2 3"

Lively (♩=210)

Irish

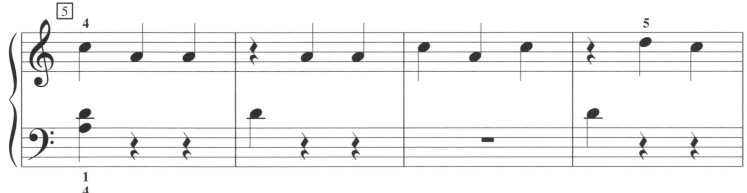

Play 1st time only. **Play 2nd time.**

1. 2.

45

Go For The Gold

Stately March

Phillip Keveren

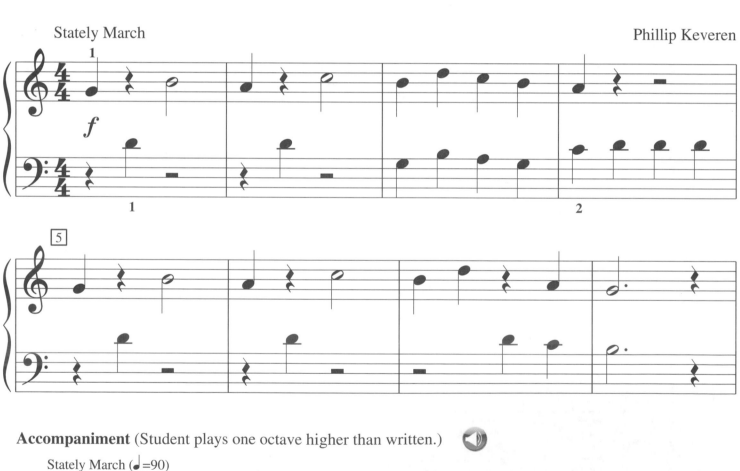

Accompaniment (Student plays one octave higher than written.)

Stately March (♩=90)

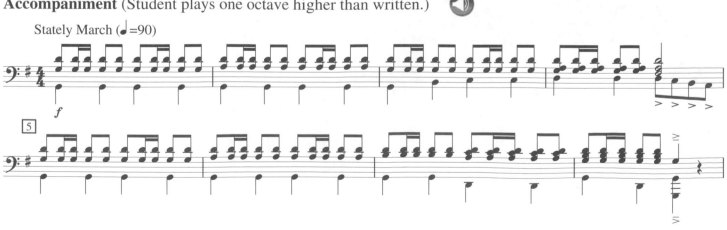

HAS SUCCESSFULLY COMPLETED
HAL LEONARD PIANO LESSONS,
BOOK TWO
AND
IS HEREBY PROMOTED TO
BOOK THREE.

TEACHER   DATE

HAL•LEONARD®